CW01261478

DEAR SISTER
from you to me

A JOURNAL OF A LIFETIME

Dear

This journal is a gift with a twist . . . it's from you to me.

When we are children we are always asking questions . . . well now I have some more for you. Please could you answer them in the way that only you know how and then give the book back to me.

There might be a couple of questions that you would prefer not to answer, so don't worry, just answer the others as well as you can . . . I won't mind.

People say that we all have at least one book in us and this will be one of yours. The story of you and me that I will treasure forever.

Thank you,

with love

Tell me about the time and place you were born . . .

What are your earliest memories?

Tell me about your childhood . . .

What do you think people thought about you as a child?

What do you remember about the place/s you lived when you were young?

What were your favourite childhood toys or games?

Tell me about your best childhood friend/s . . .

What do you remember about any holidays you had when you were young?

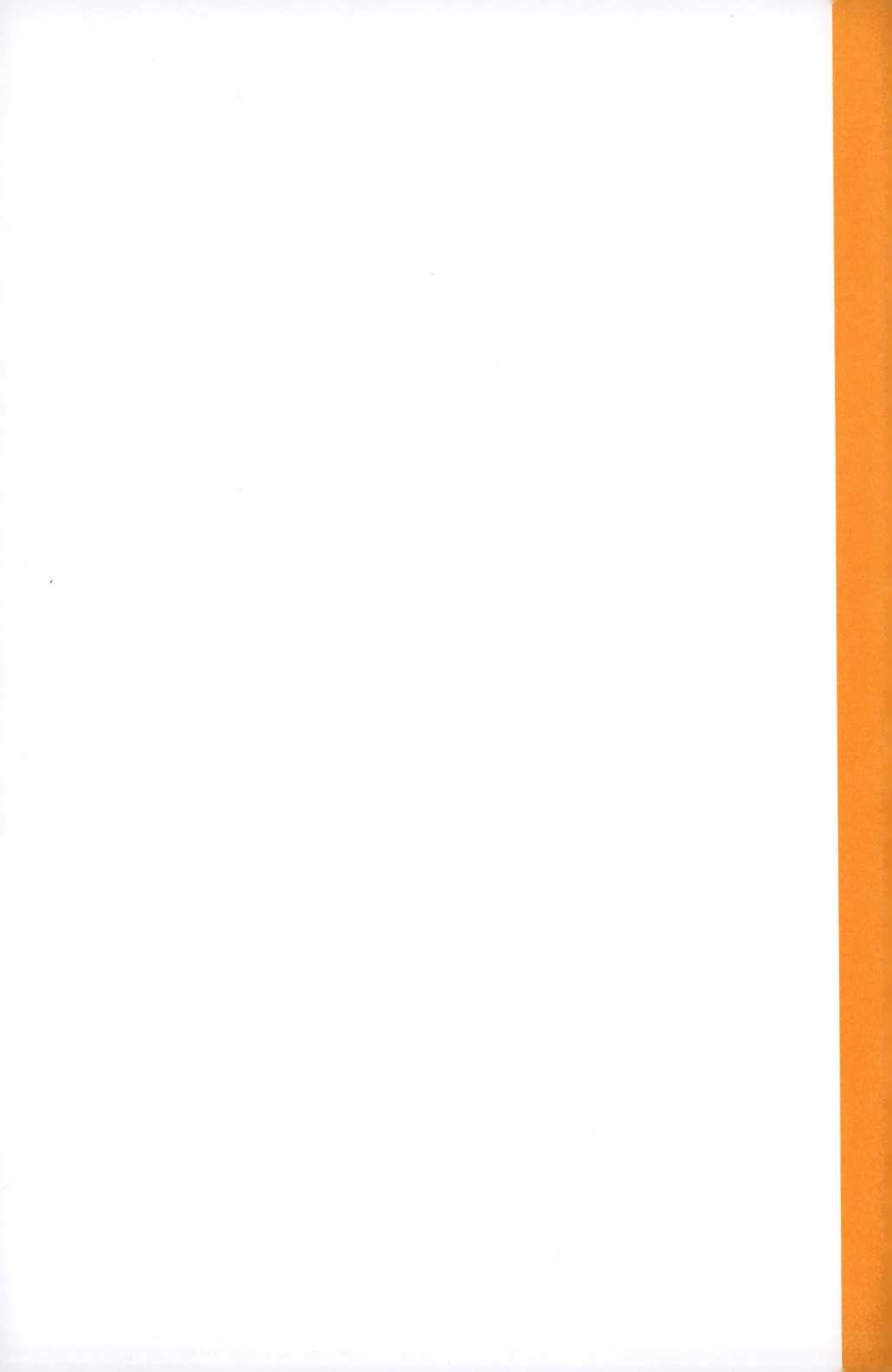

What did you enjoy about your school / college days?

What did you want to do when you grew up?

Tell me about the hobbies you had when you were young . . .

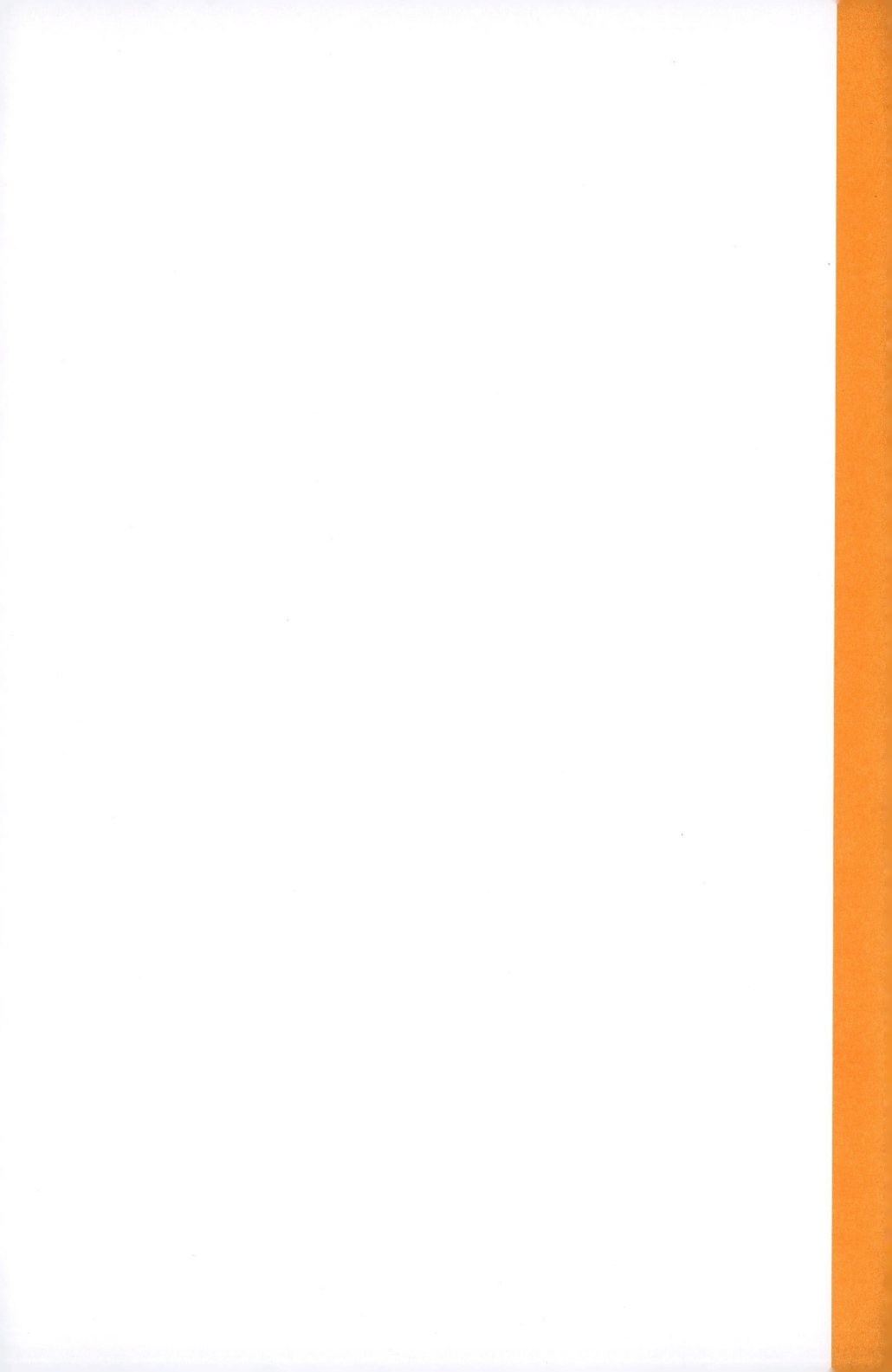

Being the eldest, youngest or a middle sibling can be different. Describe what it is like for you . . .

If you could, what would you swap with me?

What family values have you learnt that you would like to pass on to others?

Tell me some of your favourite family stories . . .

What family traditions do you continue to follow?

Did you have an idol when you were young?
Tell me who and why . . .

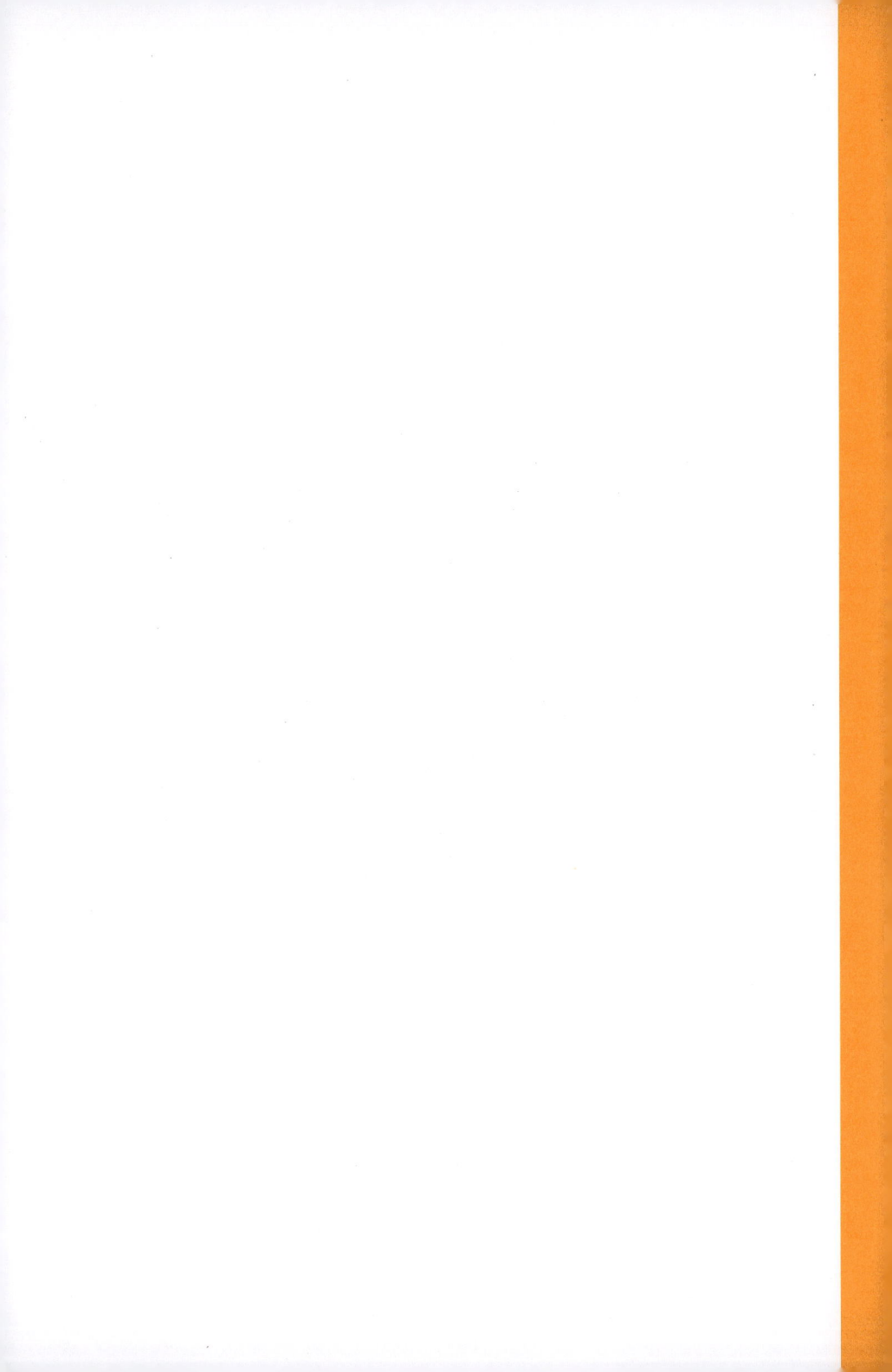

Who was your first love and why?

What was the first piece of music you bought and in what format?

Tell me about your first job and some of the other work you have done . . .

Describe some of your fondest memories of the times we have spent together . . .

Describe the funniest things that have happened to us . . .

Tell me what you like about me . . .

What is the most annoying thing I have done?

Is there anything you would change about me?

What will you remember me for?

What would you still love us to do together?

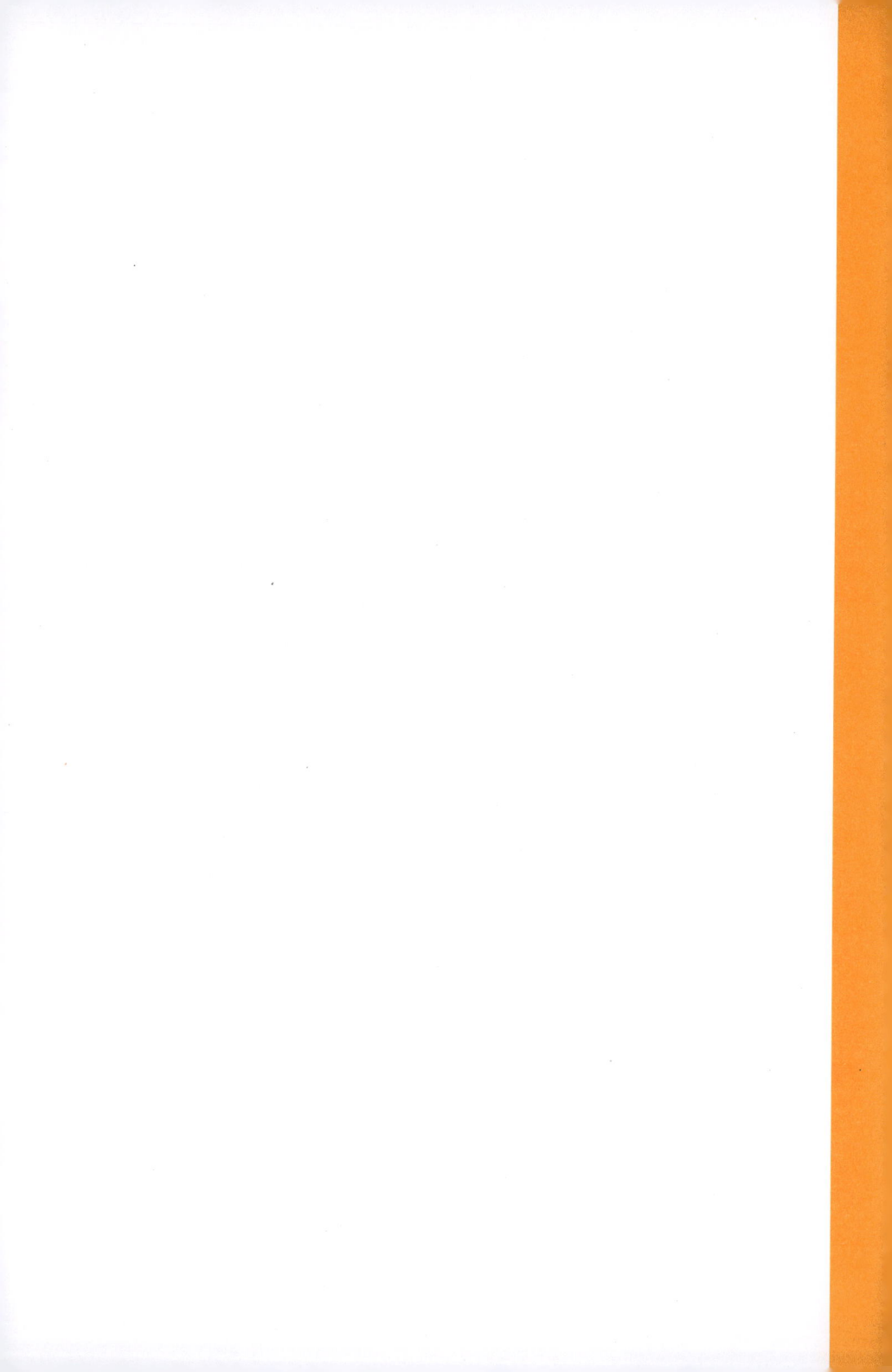

What are the happiest or greatest memories of your life?

Tell me about the things that make you happy or laugh . . .

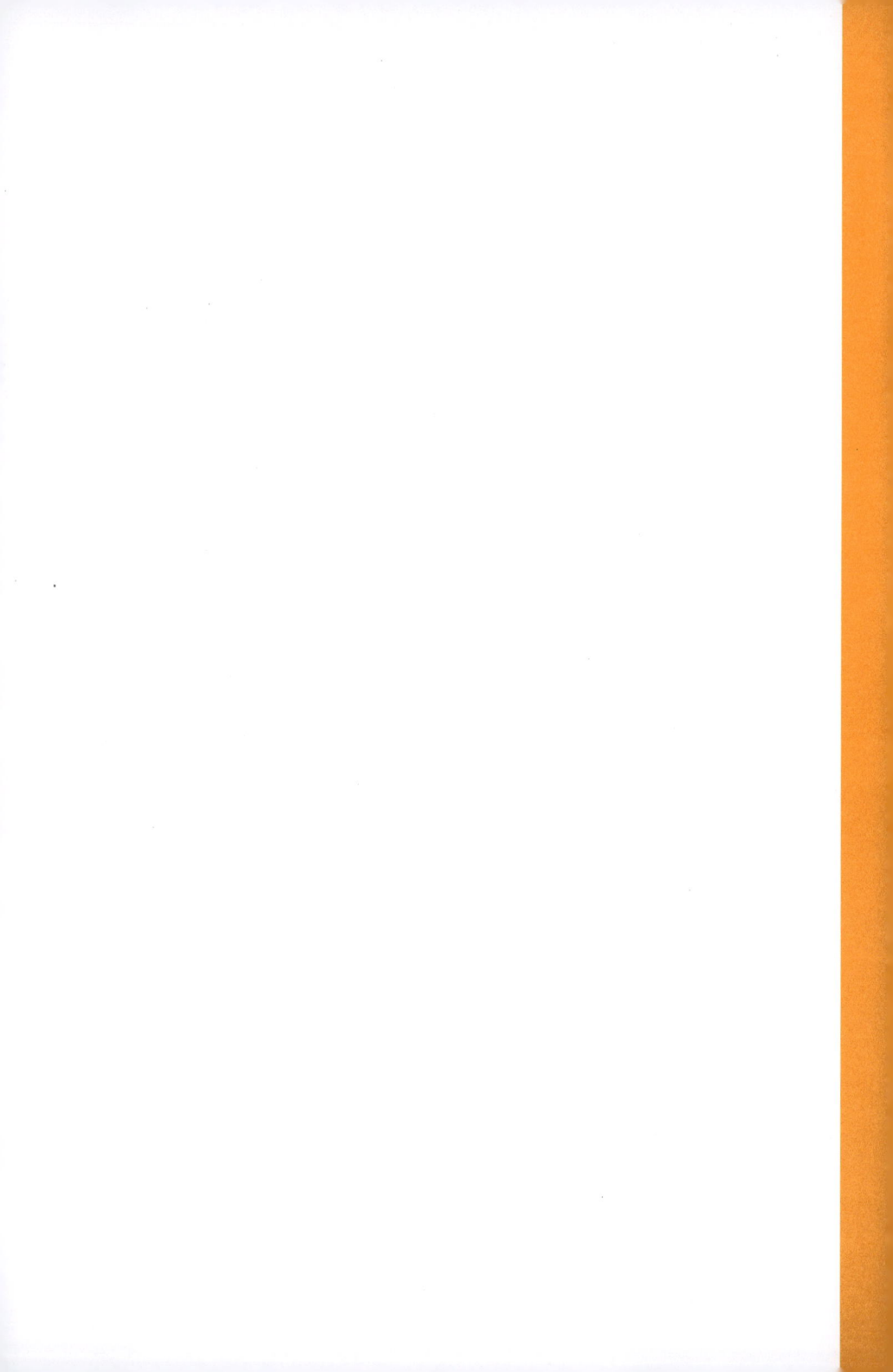

What piece/s of music would you choose to be in your 'top 10' favourite tracks?

Tell me what would make up your favourite meal . . .

Describe your favourite way of spending a weekend . . .

What would you include in your top 10 views in the world?

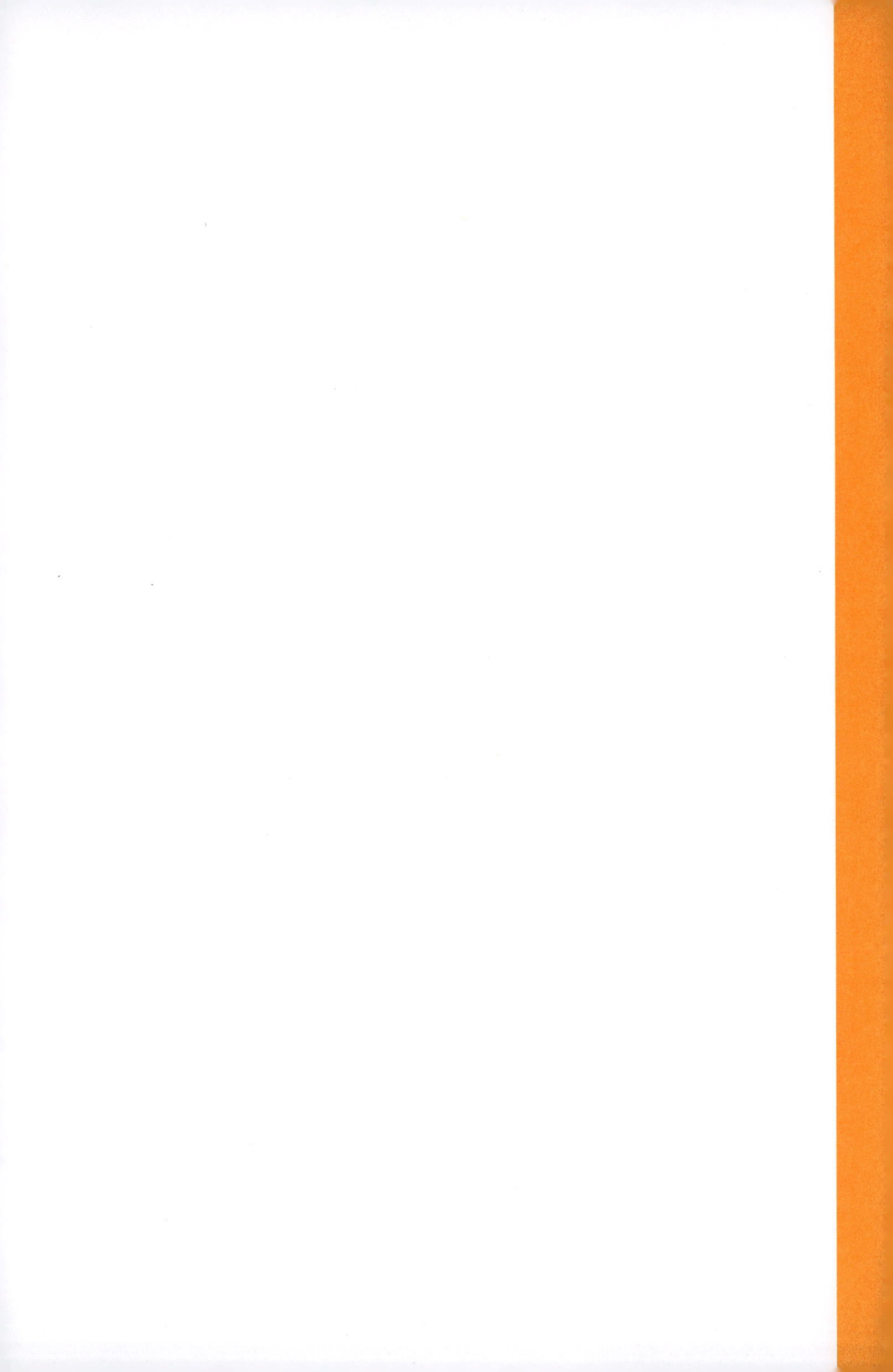

What have been some of your best holiday destinations?

If you could live anywhere . . . where would you live and why?

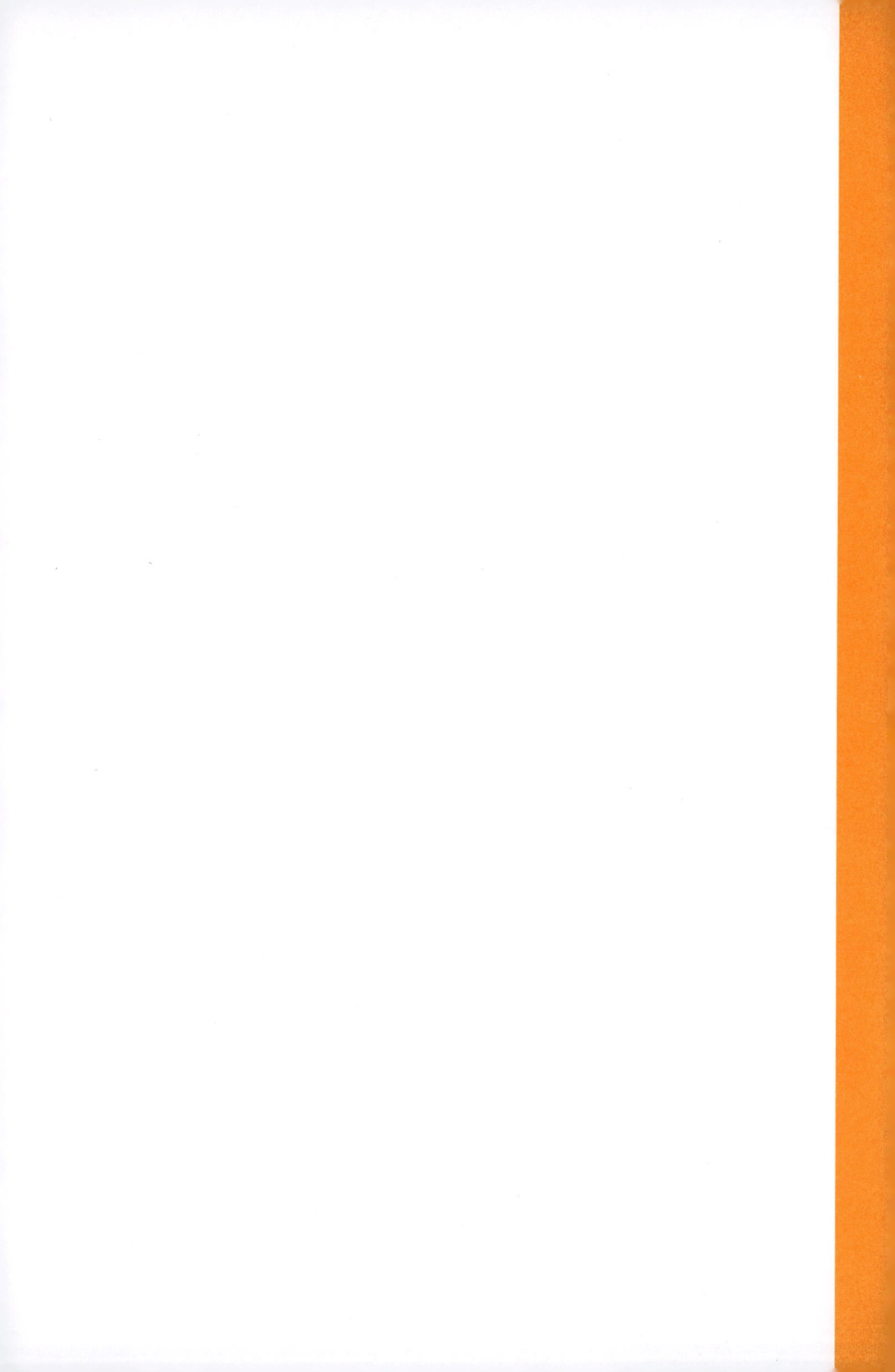

What are a few of your favourite things?

Describe your memory of some major world events that have happened in your lifetime . . .

If you could travel in time... where would you go and why?

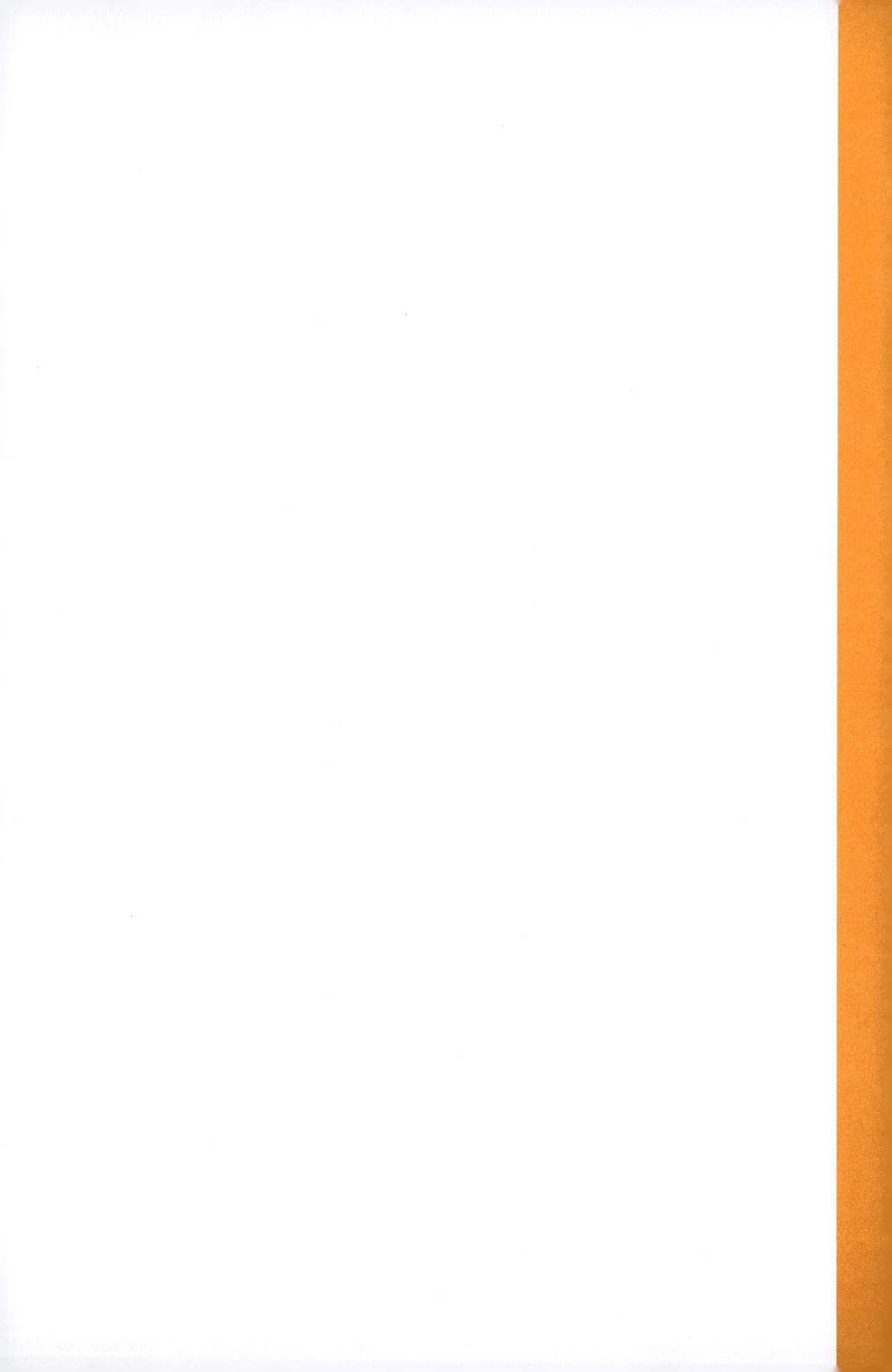

Describe the greatest changes that you have seen in your lifetime so far . . .

If you were an animal . . . what type of animal would you be, and why?

If you won the Lottery . . . what would you do with the money?

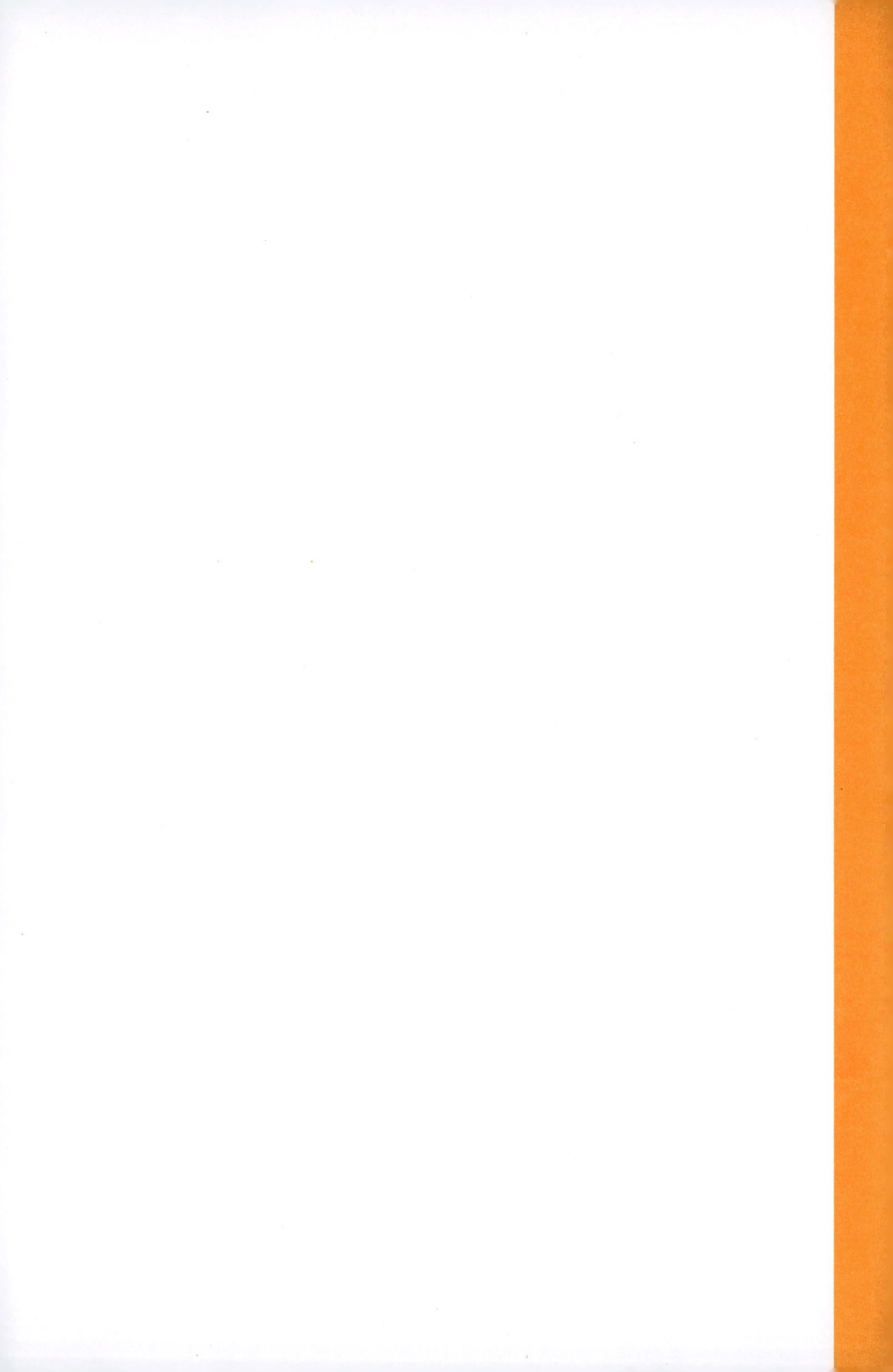

Tell me about the goals and aspirations you have had for your life . . .

What do you still want to achieve in your life?

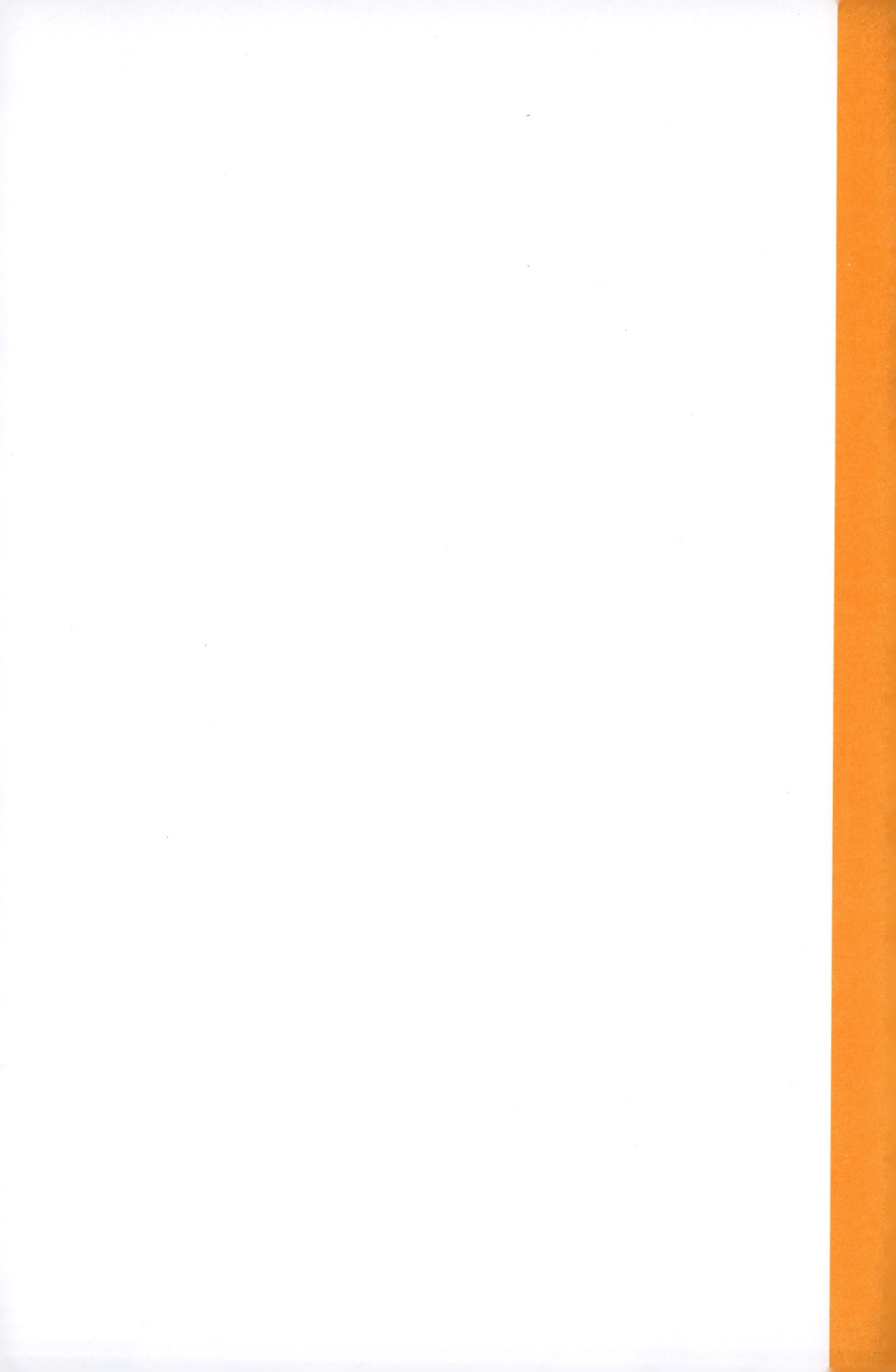

Is there anything you'd like to change about yourself?

Tell me about the dreams you have for your life . . .

What can I do to help you achieve what you want?

What have you found most difficult in your life?

What regrets do you have in your life?

Can you do anything about them now?

Is there anything you would like to say sorry for?

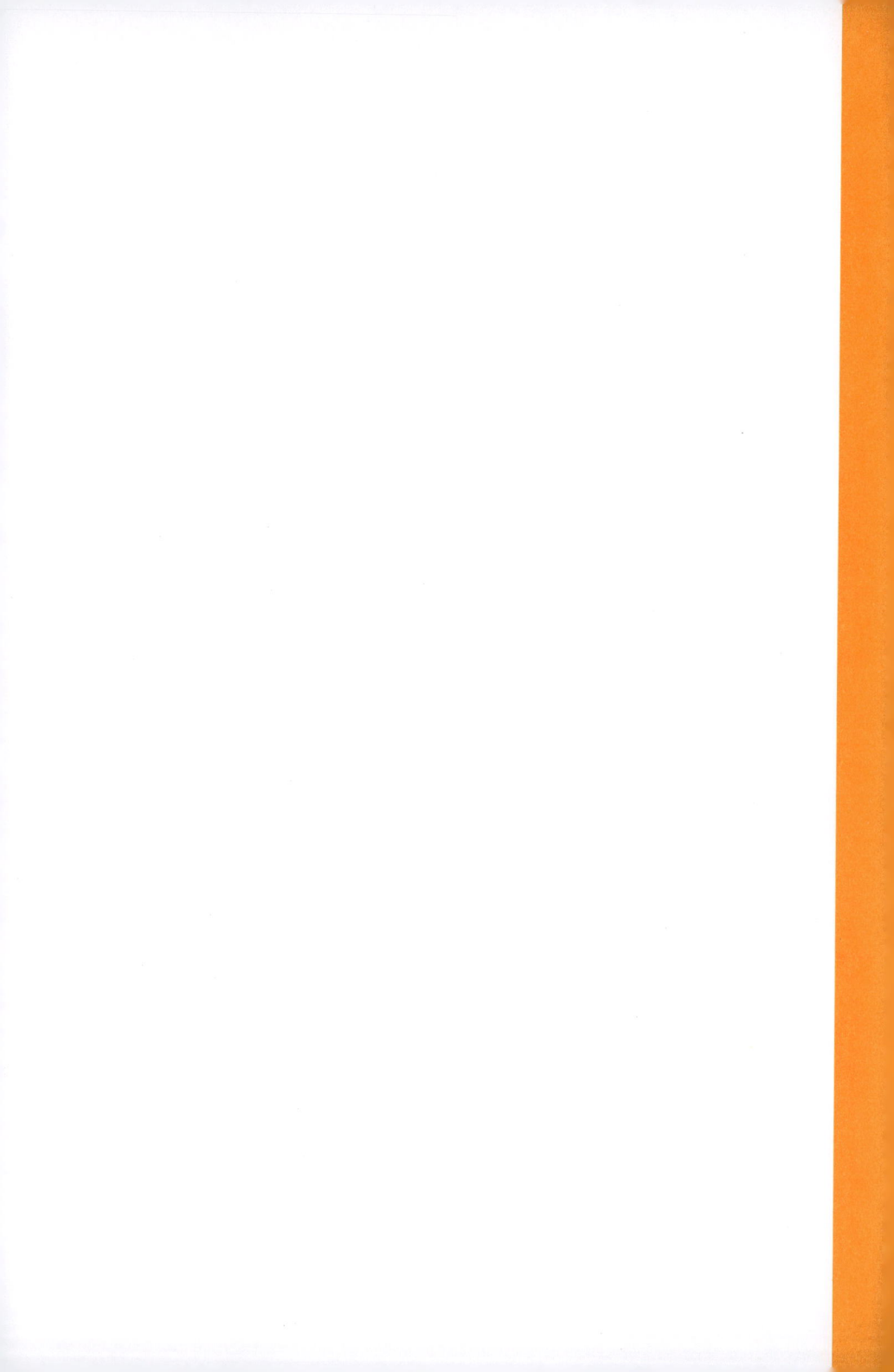

With hindsight what would you do differently?

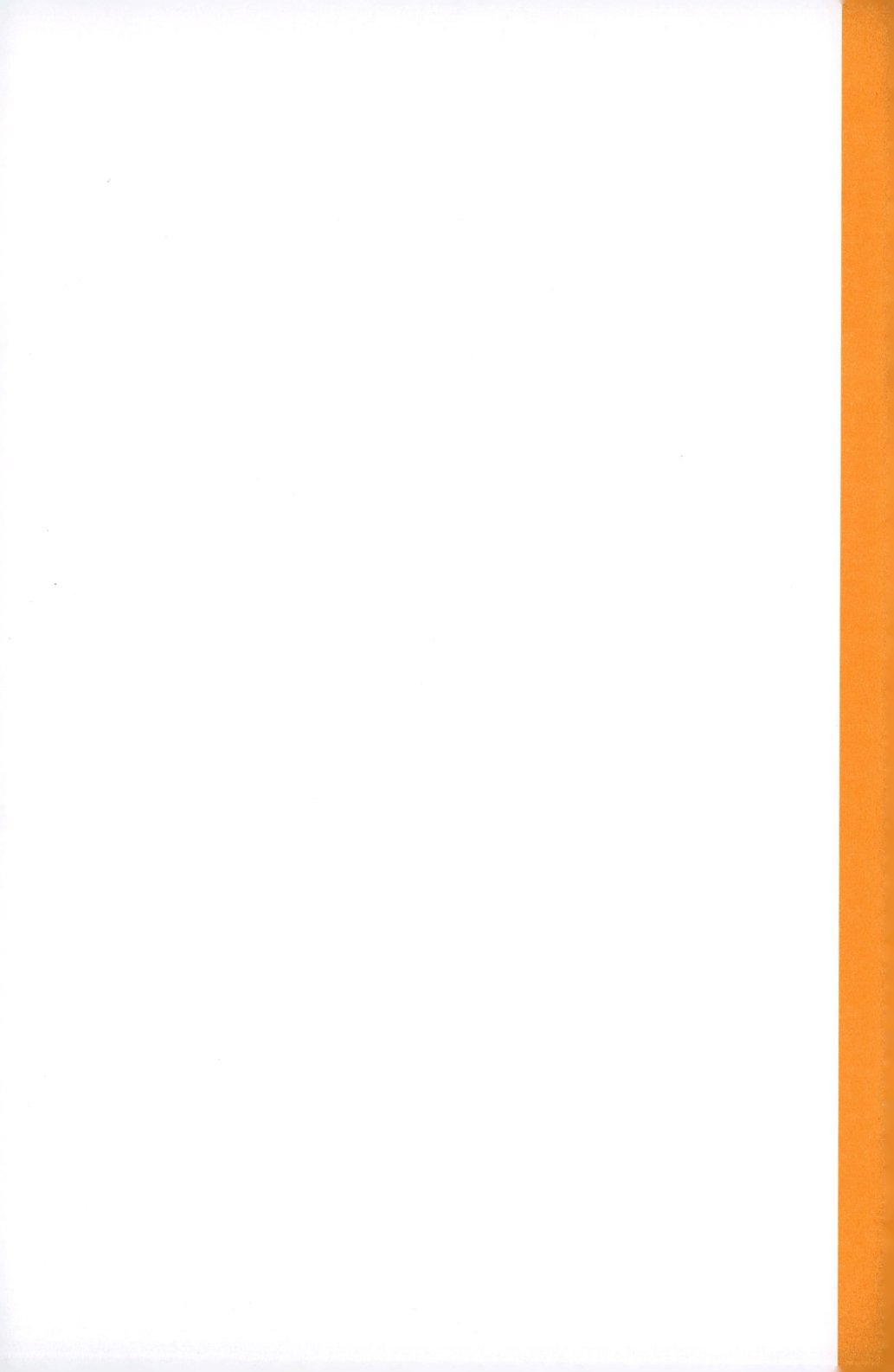

If you were granted three wishes . . . what would they be and why?

Tell me something you think I won't know about you . . .

How do you like to be thought of by others?

What is the best piece of advice you have ever been given?

Given your experiences, what advice would you like to offer me?

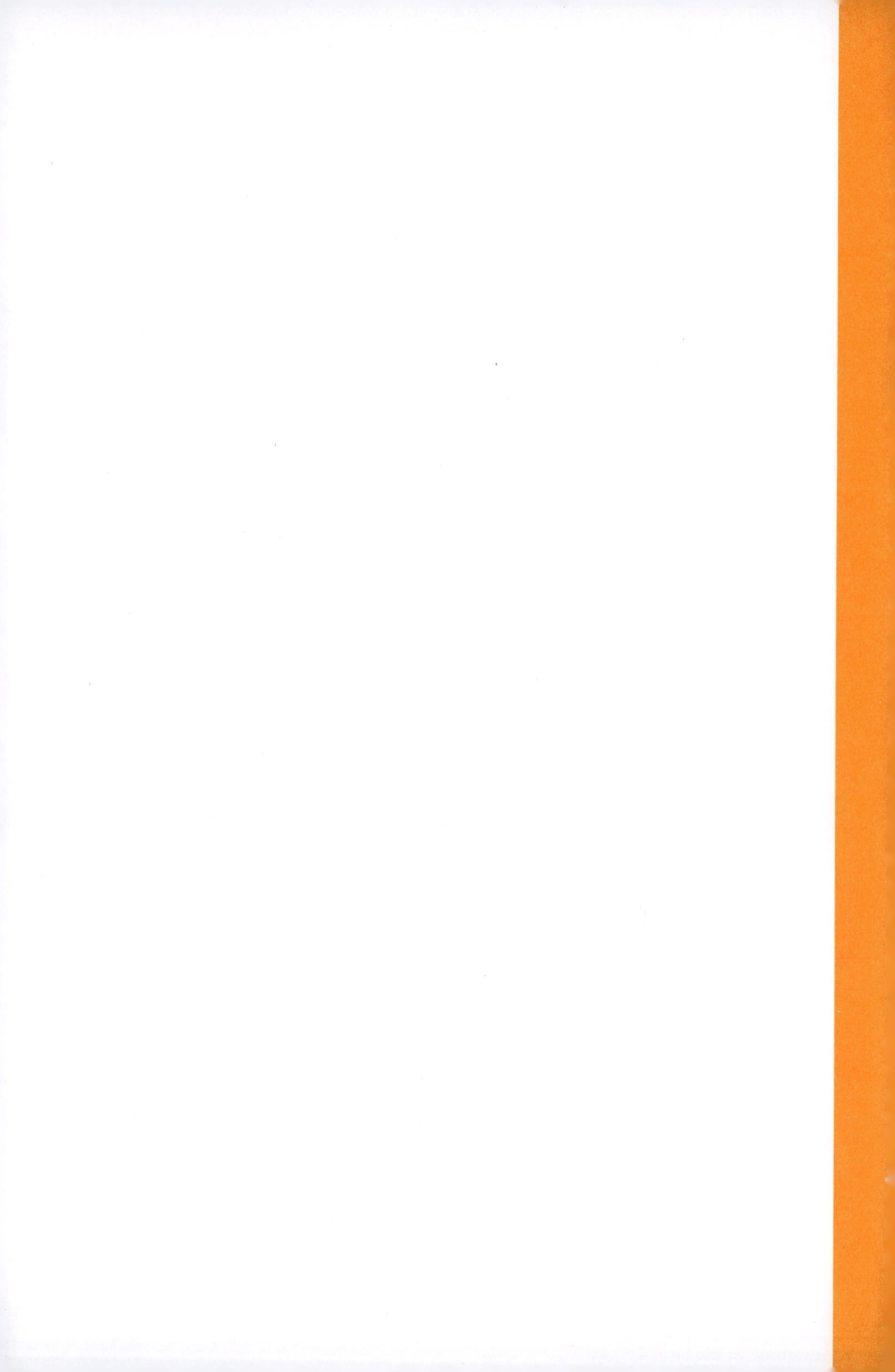

And now your chance to write anything else you want to say to me . . .

AND FINALLY FOR THE RECORD...

What is your full name?

What is your date of birth?

What colour are your eyes?

How tall are you?

What blood group are you?

What date did you complete this story for me?

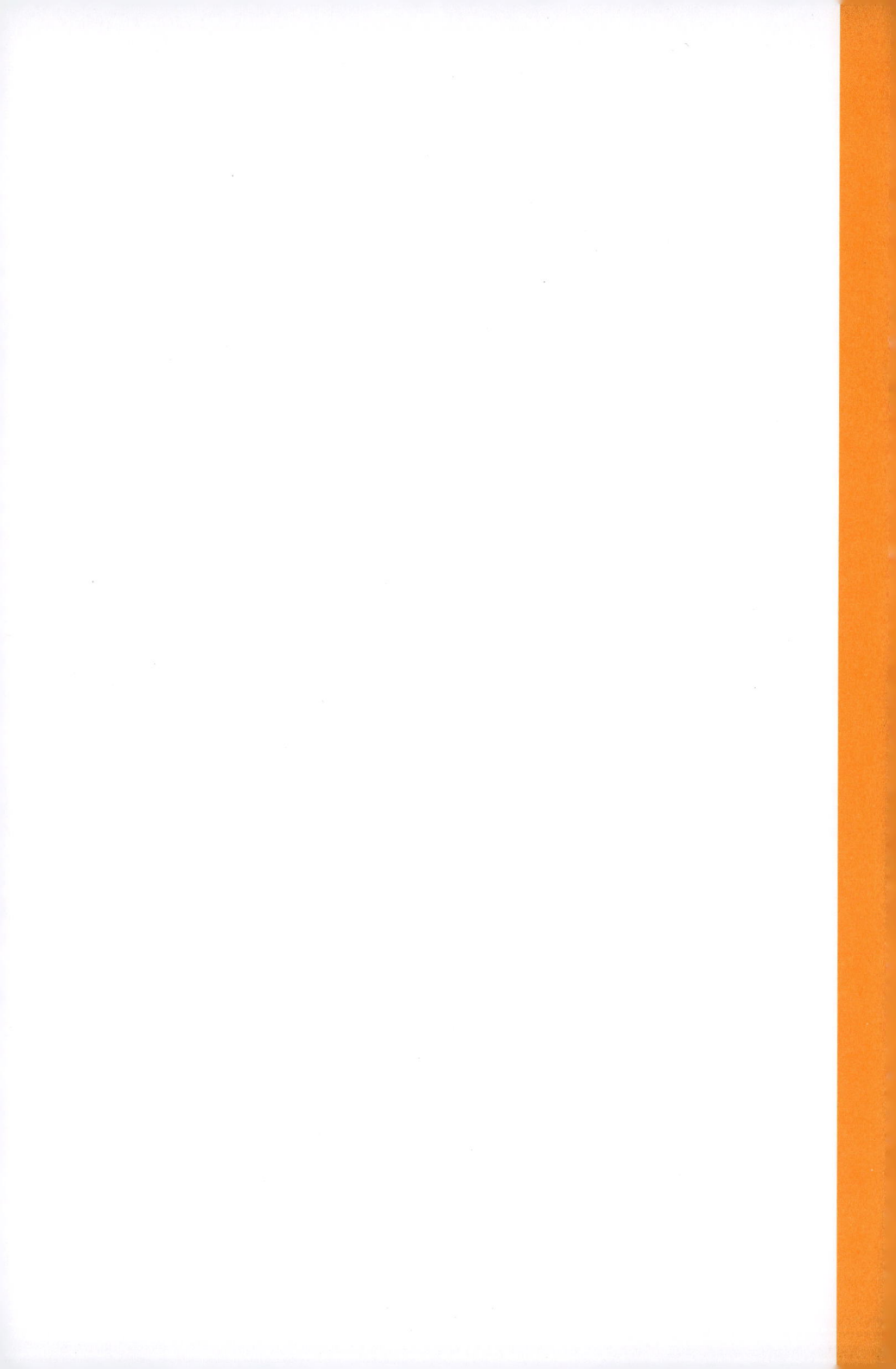

THANK YOU

for taking the time to complete this journal.
I will treasure it forever.

DEAR SISTER
from you to me©

The Timeless Collection, first published by **FROM YOU TO ME LTD** in September 2017

There are nine titles in the collection:
Dear Mum, Dad, Grandma, Grandad, Daughter, Son, Sister, Brother and Friend.

For a full range of all our titles where gifts can also be personalised, please visit

WWW.FROMYOUTOME.COM

FROM YOU TO ME are committed to a sustainable future for our business, our customers and our planet. This book is printed and bound in China on FSC® certified paper.

MIX
Paper | Supporting responsible forestry
FSC® C005748

All rights reserved. No part of this publication may be reproduced, stored in a retrieval system, or transmitted in any form or by any means electronic, mechanical, photocopying, recording, or otherwise, without the prior written permission of the copyright owner who can be contacted via the publisher at the above website address.

3 5 7 9 11 13 15 14 12 10 8 6 4

Copyright © 2017 **FROM YOU TO ME LTD**

ISBN 978-1-907860-34-8

FROM YOU TO ME LTD, STUDIO 100, THE OLD LEATHER FACTORY
GLOVE FACTORY STUDIOS, HOLT, WILTSHIRE, BA14 6RJ

ISBN 978-1-907860-34-8